This edition published 2018

Copyright 2018 Anya Acres

The right of Anya Acres to be identified as author
respectively of this work has been asserted by her,
in accordance with the Copyright, Design and Patents Act 1988.

All rights reserved. No part of this publication may be
reproduced, stored in retrieval system, or transmitted in any form
or by any means, electronic, mechanical, photocopy, recording
or other wise without the prior permission of the author.

ISBN 978-1-9999526-1-7

Happy reading ... A.Acres

www.olliediscovers.co.uk

To my wonderful sons, Ollie and James.
You make me the proudest mum on Earth!

Triceratops

T-Rex

Brontosaurus

Can you find all of the missing dinosaurs?

Stegosaurus

Pterodactyl

Ollie discovers... the DINOSAURS

By
Anya Acres

Illustrated by
Filip Lazurowicz

This here is Ollie,
He has a big smile.
He'd like an adventure,
It's been a while . . .

EARTH

ENGINE

TURBO

BRAKE

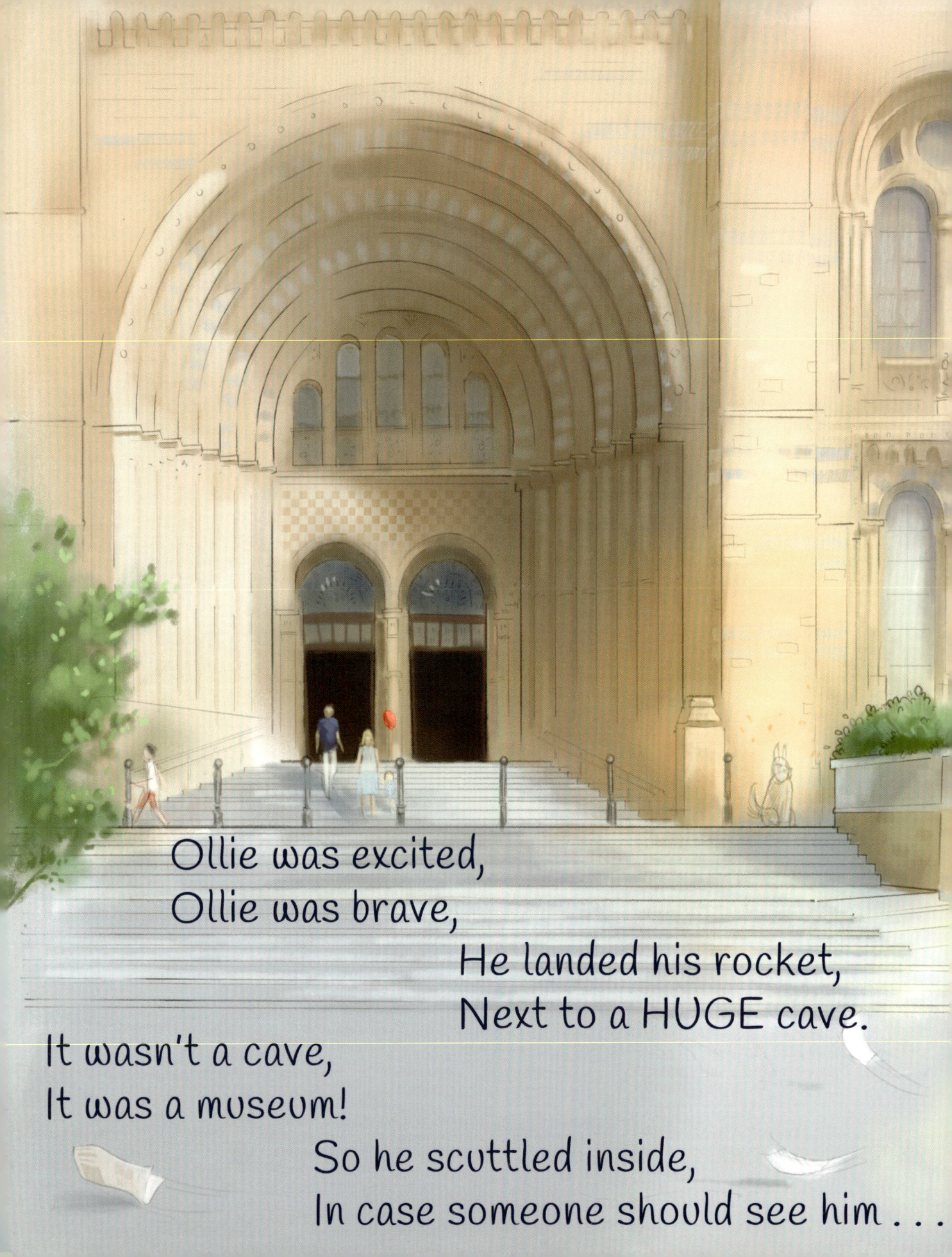

Ollie was excited,
Ollie was brave,
He landed his rocket,
Next to a HUGE cave.
It wasn't a cave,
It was a museum!
So he scuttled inside,
In case someone should see him . . .

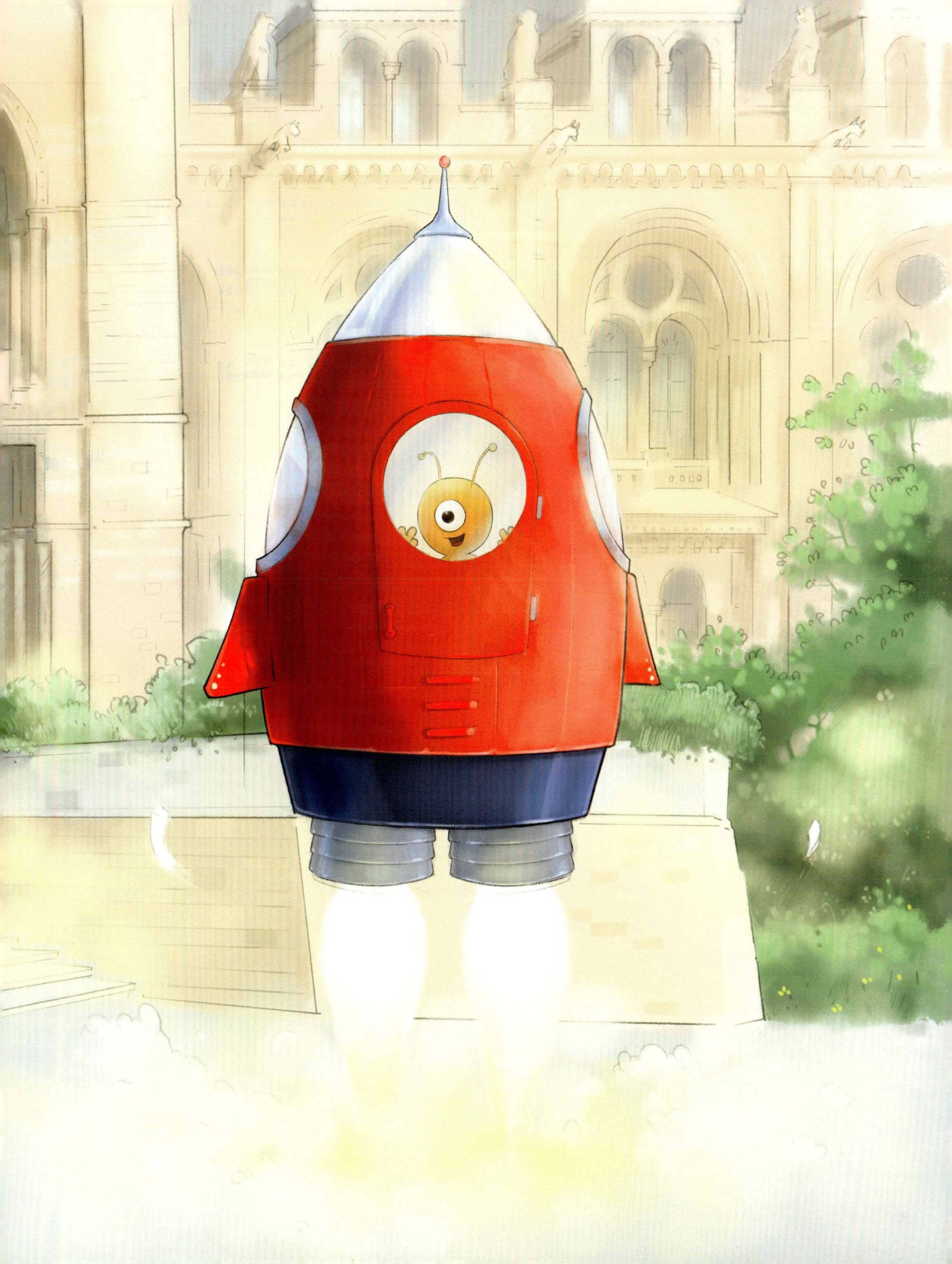

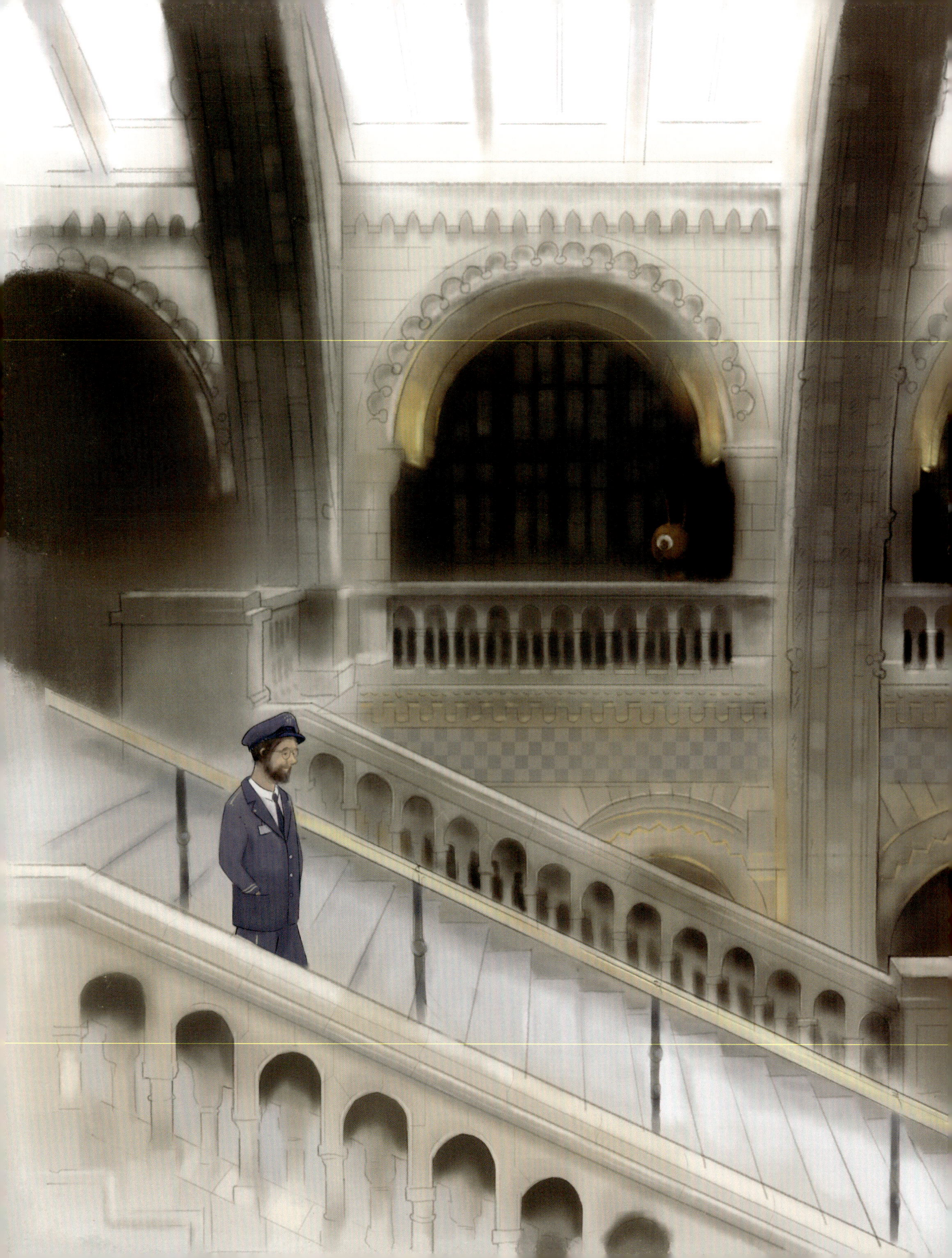

He was lonely and scared,
In the gloomy museum.
So he tip-toed through shadows,
So no one could see him . . .

This here is James,
He's a boy with a frown.
He lost his five dinos,
When they fell on the ground.

James went on a trip,
But his bag had a rip.
So his five dinosaurs,
Fell onto the floor.

James hid,
When his teacher went onto the bus.
He missed his five dinos,
So didn't make a fuss.

He hid beneath shadows,
In the gloomy museum.
He waited 'til dark,
So no one could see him.

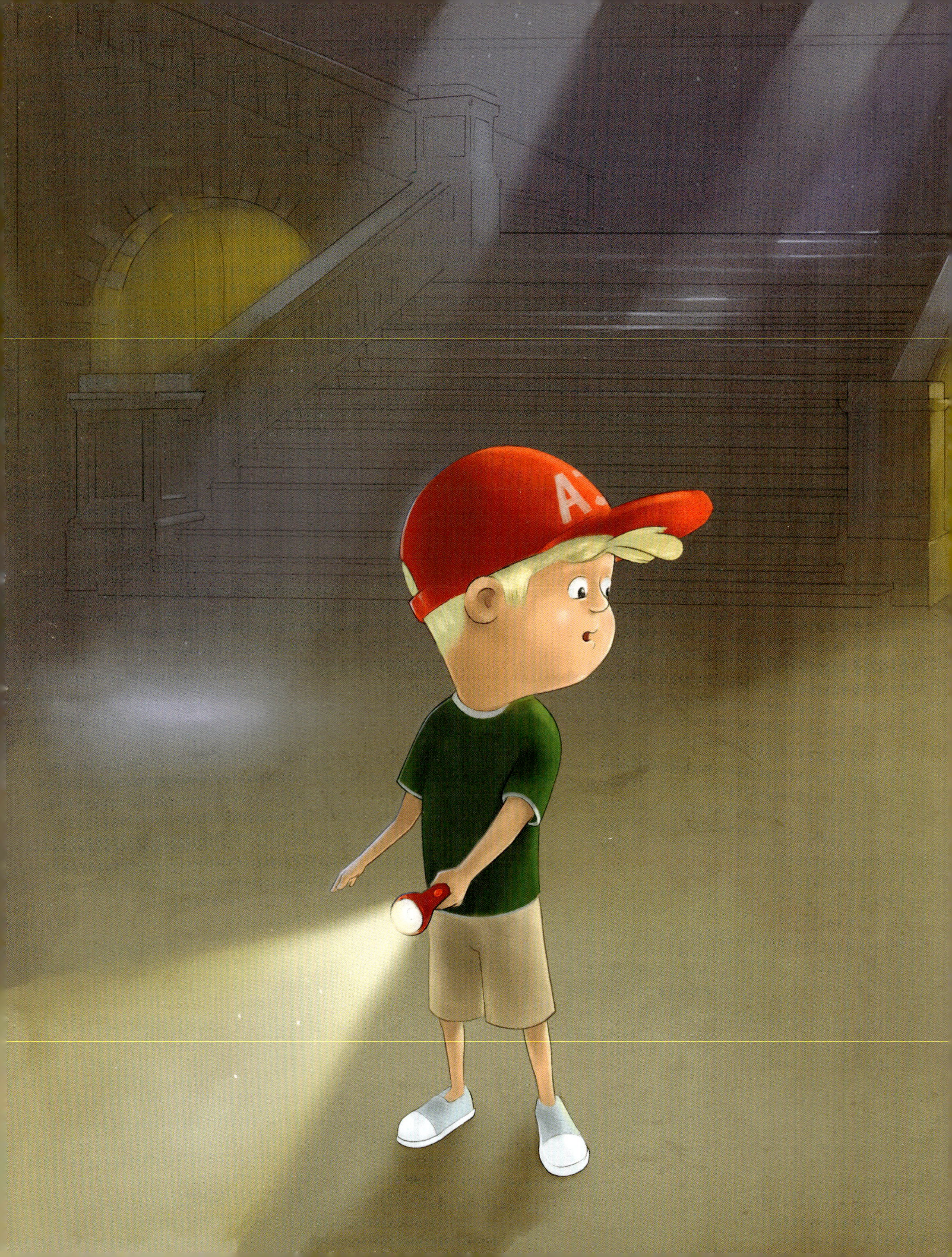

James searched for his dinos,
For quite some while.
Then out of the shadows,
He spotted a smile.

It was Ollie!
And a hand he would lend.
To find the five dinos,
Was the job of a friend.

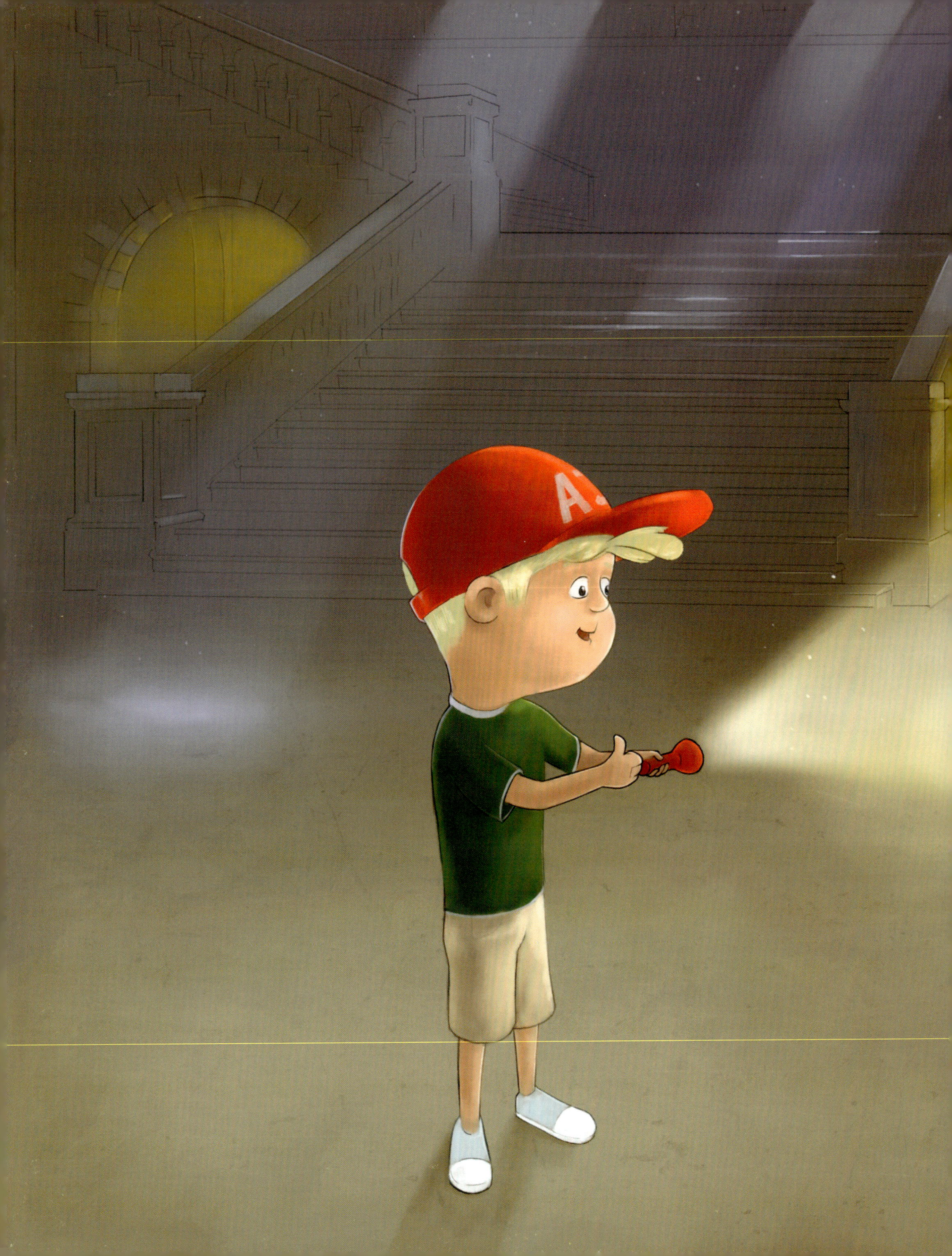

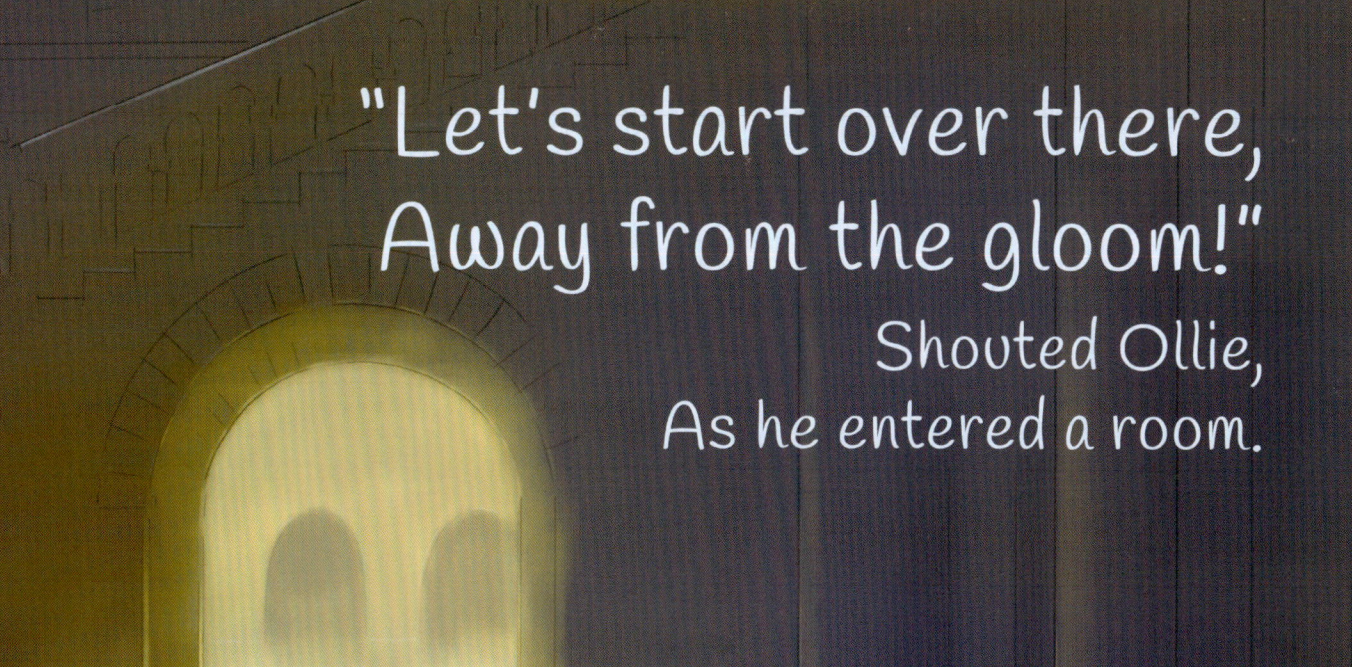

"Let's start over there,
Away from the gloom!"
Shouted Ollie,
As he entered a room.

They saw a T-rex, with fierce looking claws,
Tiny small hands, and a terrible jaw.

Then there in the corner, all covered in dirt,
Was a blue dinosaur ... Let's hope it's not hurt!

"Hurrah", giggled James,
"I have one dinosaur!"
As the moon cast a shadow,
On the museum floor.

It lived in North America

It was a carnivore

It had two clawed digits and a long heavy tail

It could measure up to 6 metres tall, and 12 metres long

"A Triceratops!"
Shouted James in delight!

"Look at his three horns,
He's ready to fight!"

Then there in the corner
All covered in dirt,
Was a green dinosaur
Let's hope it's not hurt!

It lived in North America

It was a herbivore

It had a three-horned face

It could measure up to 3 metres tall and 9 metres long

"Hurrah," chuckled James, "I have two dinosaurs!"
As the moon cast a shadow, On the museum floors.

A dino with wings???
Could that be true?
"It's a Pterodactyl" said James,
"Without mine, I feel blue."

It lived in Europe & Africa

It was a carnivore

It was a flying reptile

It's wing span could measure up to 1 metre

Then there in the corner
All covered in dirt,
Was a red dinosaur . . .
Let's hope it's not hurt!

"Hurrah", shrieked James,
"I have three dinosaurs!"
As the moon cast a shadow,
On the museum floors.

They saw a Brontosaurus,
With a very long neck.
"It's a herbivore" said James,
"Many plants it would wreck."

It lived in North America

It was a herbivore

It had a long thin neck and a small head

It was 4.5 metres tall and 27 metres long

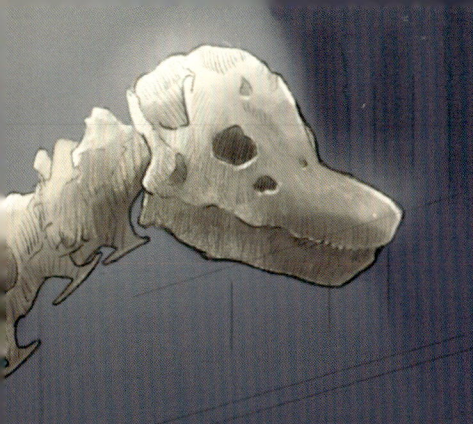

Then there in the corner,
All covered in dirt,
Was a pink dinosaur . . .
Let's hope it's not hurt!

"Hurrah", smiled James,
"I have four dinosaurs!"
As the moon cast a shadow,
On the museum floors.

"I see a Stegosaurus,
With plates down it's back.
A very small head,
He's ready to attack!"

- It lived in Western America and Portugal
- It was a herbivore
- It had broad upright plates and a tail tipped with spikes
- It was 2.5 metres tall and 9 metres long

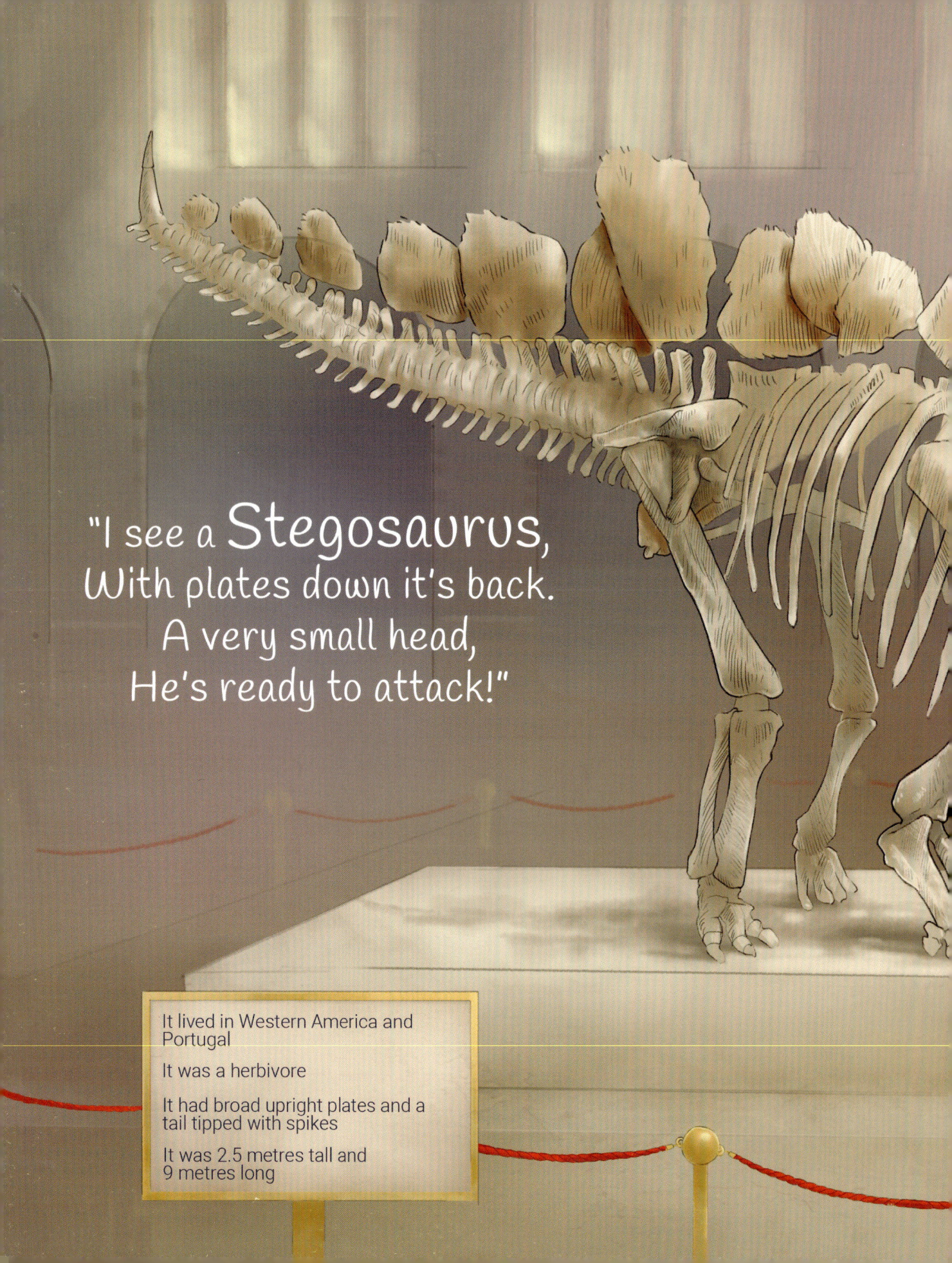

Then there in the corner
All covered in dirt,
Was a purple dinosaur . . .
Let's hope it's not hurt!

"Hurrah", beamed James,
"I have my five dinosaurs!"
As the sun began rising;
Casting light on the floors.

James looked at the clock,
"It's time to go home,
But how will I get there?"
Said James with a groan.

"Jump in my rocket,
And to home we will fly!"
Then his heart filled with sorrow,
When he thought of goodbye.

James smiled down at Ollie,
"Our friendship won't end!
When I think of the fun,
I've had with my friend."

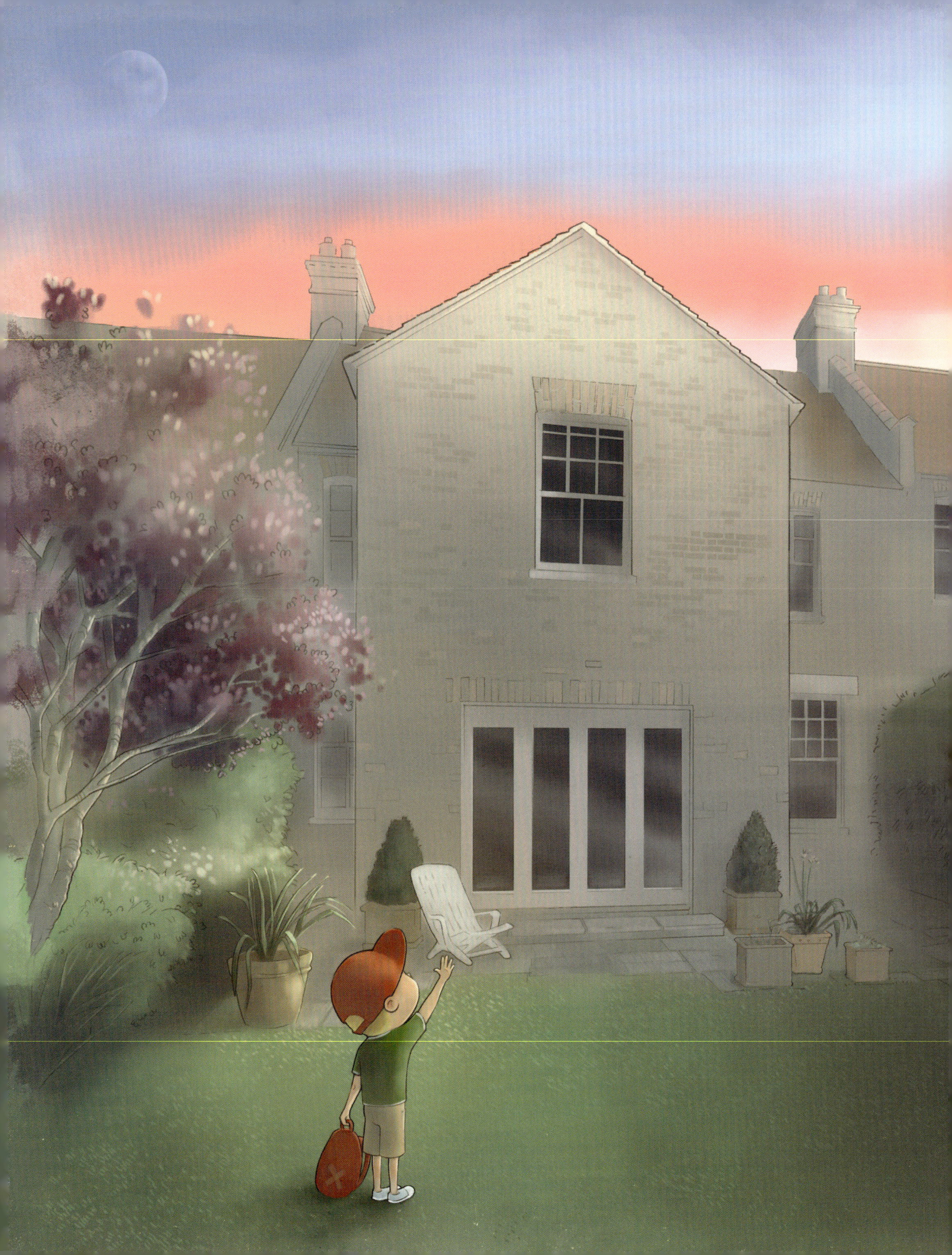

The moon sank low, and faded,
As the sun rose in the sky.
Their frowns had turned to laughter,
As they waved a last goodbye.

Dinosaur Quiz

1. What do the words herbivore and carnivore mean?

2. Why do you think the T-rex had only two legs?

3. Where did the Triceratops live?

4. Why do you think the Brontosaurus had such a long neck?

5. Dinosaurs became extinct many, many years ago; where would you find a dinosaur now, and why?